*plan your wedding gift list
essentials

paula onslow

foulsham
LONDON • NEW YORK • TORONTO • SYDNEY

foulsham
The Publishing House, Bennetts Close,
Cippenham, Slough, Berks, SL1 5AP, England

ISBN 0-572-02962-4

Copyright © 2004 W. Foulsham & Co. Ltd

Cover photograph © The Image Bank

A CIP record for this book is available from the British Library

All rights reserved.

The Copyright Act prohibits (subject to certain very limited exceptions) the making of copies of any copyright work or of a substantial part of such a work, including the making of copies by photocopying or similar process. Written permission to make a copy or copies must therefore normally be obtained from the publisher in advance. It is advisable to consult the publisher if in any doubt as to the legality of any copying which is to be undertaken.

While every effort has been made to ensure the accuracy of all the information contained within this book, neither the author nor the publisher can be liable for any errors. In particular, since laws change from time to time, it is vital that each individual should check relevant legal details for themselves.

Printed in Great Britain by Cox & Wyman Ltd, Reading

Contents

	Introduction	5
Chapter 1	Should You Have a Wedding Gift List?	7
Chapter 2	Choosing Where to Have Your Wedding Gift List	11
Chapter 3	Letting Your Guests Know You Have a Wedding Gift List	23
Chapter 4	Keeping Your List Up to Date	26
Chapter 5	Thank-you Letters	29
Chapter 6	How to Plan Your Wedding Gift List	33
Chapter 7	Choosing Your Wedding Presents	41
Chapter 8	Finalising Your Wedding Gift List	79
Chapter 9	Delivery and Gift Wrapping	82
Chapter 10	What to Do if Your Wedding is Cancelled	88
Chapter 11	With the Benefit of Hindsight	90
Chapter 12	Your Wedding Gift List	95
	Wedding Gift List Companies	124
	Index	127

Introduction

Love them or hate them, wedding gift lists have become one of the major aspects of wedding planning in recent years. Many people think that they are a relatively new idea but that's not the case. I know a couple who, when they married in the 1950s, had their list at Peter Jones and General Trading Company. So wedding gift lists are very well established and are almost an expected part of the wedding.

Nowadays, though, an increasing number of couples already have their own flat or house, or are living together before they marry, so the idea of the wedding gifts being entirely to help the young couple equip their first home as they leave their parents' homes is very much out of date. In some ways, this makes wedding lists even more essential. A few decades ago a couple might well have been given the notorious two toasters, but now you could already have one each and then receive two more as wedding gifts!

Some brides say they don't have time to organise a wedding gift list because they have too much else to do, what with choosing their dress, the flowers, the hymns and the menus and organising everything else involved with the wedding. There's a lot of truth in that, but it's important to think about your wedding gifts as a longer-term investment, and on your tenth

Introduction

wedding anniversary – when your wedding day has become a happy memory and an album of photographs that spends most of its time in a cupboard – the gifts you received from family and friends will still be a constant reminder of your big day. Looked at in that way, I think there is a good case for spending a little time managing your wedding present list.

Then you can consider it from your guests' point of view. If *you* want to receive presents you need and will enjoy, *they* equally want to be sure that they spend their time, effort and money on a gift they can be sure you need and will really appreciate.

The average couple receives £3,000 worth of wedding gifts. Imagine £3,000 of presents that you haven't chosen yourself. Think of your aunt who, without being pointed in the right direction, will tend to give you something *she* likes; much as you love her, do you really share her tastes? Or you might have invited some friends, a wonderfully outrageous couple with an unconventional and quirky lifestyle; who knows what they might give you if left to their own devices? Now think of £3,000 spent on the items you have carefully chosen to make your new house into the home you would like it to be. I rest my case.

There are various options, of course, as to how you organise your list and these are covered in the chapters that follow. But even if you only compile a list and give it to your mother so that she can suggest what you might like when people ask, it is far better than leaving the whole present issue to complete pot luck.

Chapter 1
Should You Have a Wedding Gift List?

Even people who can see the logic of having a wedding gift list often feel very awkward about it, so the first thing to do is to make sure you are comfortable with the concept of a wedding gift list. Then you can decide how to organise it so that everyone gets the best from the situation.

There is no point spending ages compiling a list and then being so embarrassed about it that when someone asks you what you would like as a wedding present you just say, 'Oh anything you would like to give us would be great'. If you give it a little thought in advance, you can make it work for everyone.

Am I being greedy?

Some people feel that it looks greedy and presumptuous to compile a list of presents they would like to receive and believe that it is better just to accept whatever presents their wedding guests choose to give them. At the other end of the scale, of course, there are those who feel no guilt whatsoever and just think of absolutely everything they could ever possibly want or need in their married life and list it all down, from mundane household items to vast quantities of china, glass and cutlery, expensive kitchen equipment, linen, lamps, rugs and major items of furniture. I like to think there's a happy medium!

The aim when choosing any gift is to find something the recipient needs or will really like. When there are many people all trying to achieve that for one couple, it's highly likely that some of them are going to hit on the same things. The result: disappointment or inconvenience for the couple, who have things they don't need but don't have things they do; and disappointment for the guests when they realise that their gift is not quite the success they had envisaged.

List or no list, your friends and family will want to give you presents, and you will be amazed at how generous people are – at the time of writing, the average guest spends £83 on a wedding present. Everyone concerned will want that money to be well spent and the gift appreciated so, far from being greedy, it is sensible and considerate to direct your guests towards what you might like.

Make sure your parents are happy

The bride's mother in particular is likely to be heavily involved in organising the list, so it is also very important that she, and the groom's parents, are happy with the idea. Involve them in the decision-making and the planning and they will soon be as convinced as you are about the advantages, and that will make them happy to talk about the list to family and friends.

Setting the boundaries

We'll go into a lot more detail later on about what you might like to include on your wedding list, but at the outset it will help to have some idea of how your guests will view the expenditure involved in being invited to the wedding and how it relates to the gift list.

A wedding invitation can mean considerable expense for your guests, and my grandmother always used to say that being invited to a wedding was a dubious privilege! There's the gift, of course, but there's also the outfit, the travelling, and possibly even overnight accommodation. That makes it especially important that they feel their money has been well spent and, at least where the gift is concerned, you can make sure that is the case.

Everyone will have their individual budgets, which will vary considerably, so you also need to make sure that you include gifts with a broad range of prices so there is something for everyone to choose from.

Aunts, uncles and family friends of your parents' generation are likely to be very generous when buying presents. They may be at a stage in their lives when they have a little more cash to spare, and they probably don't go to many weddings each year so your special day will be a big event for them too. Buying you four dinner plates or a silver pepper mill they know you really want might cost as much as £100, but most older guests will feel far more comfortable with this than if they spend a smaller amount on a gift they are uncertain about.

Should You Have a Wedding Gift List?

Younger people often find themselves going to several weddings in a year and tend to have lower spending limits. Their budget might be nearer the £20–30 mark, but they will still want to make sure that they give you something you will appreciate so their money is not wasted. Perhaps you feel that your friends and cousins of around your own age could safely be encouraged to use their imagination a little. After all, every household needs a kitchen timer but it doesn't have to be everyday and boring; pedal bins and washing up bowls do come in colours other than beige. So, unless you know exactly which fruit bowl and tea towels (dish cloths), say, you want and no others will do, for some items it's a good idea to be unspecific about the choice. Within limits, it's very pleasant to have a few surprises!

Chapter 2

Choosing Where to Have Your Wedding Gift List

Once you have decided that you are going to have a wedding gift list, the next step is to decide where it's going to be held. The options are:

- A list held by your mother or chief bridesmaid
- A list held at a department store
- A list with a specialised wedding gift list company
- A list with a number of different individual shops
- A list held with an internet wedding gift list service

There are pros and cons to all the main options, so you need to look at each to decide which one suits you best.

A list held by your mother or chief bridesmaid

For this option, you simply draw up your complete list on paper or a PC for her to administer.

She can chat to people over the phone or send them copies of the list to read and choose from at their leisure. Guests then

Choosing Where to Have Your Wedding Gift List

report back what they have chosen so the master list can be kept up to date. Alternatively, she could just keep one master copy for circulation, though she will need to stress the need to return it promptly once the guest has selected so it can be passed on. Some people write the list in a spiral-bound notebook, one item per page. Then guests can simply tear out the page containing the gift they have chosen and pass the book back, or on to the next guest.

Having made their choice, the guests then visit their preferred store, buy the present and take it home to wrap it and give to you at an appropriate time.

Pros

The world is your oyster. You can include anything on the list from china and glass to a garden hose or a day's pony trekking in Wales.

It's quite informal and personal, which many guests will prefer.

Keeping it up to date on the PC is much easier than when you could only mark up a single list.

Guests can buy the gift wherever they like, so there are no geographical restrictions.

Guests will wrap their own gifts and write a personal message and you won't have to wait until after the wedding to receive your presents.

Cons

Organising the list, sending it out and keeping it up to date is quite time consuming. Your mother will be involved in many other preparations for weeks or months before the wedding and administering the list may be one task too far. Your chief bridesmaid will be less involved in the wedding in the early stages but may be more restricted for time by her job or a young family.

Most people will want to look at the complete list, so copies will have to be sent to guests. This adds postage costs if you can't e-mail the list.

To avoid duplication of gifts, the list can really only go to one person at a time, which can take time.

A list held at a department store

Many department stores run wedding gift lists. You go to the store or go online and customise its basic list, omitting items you don't want and adding the details of the items you do. Once it is complete, the store keeps the list for you. The service, which includes a personal adviser to help you, is usually provided free of charge, though some stores charge for delivery and wrapping.

Your guests then go into any branch of the store or to the website and ask to see your list. They choose from the items (you can ask the store to steer guests towards particular items, if you wish), and usually the store takes the payment for the gift and makes a note of the donor's message.

The store will keep the list up to date with who has bought what and may send you regular updates. It will arrange for delivery of all your gifts, unless you choose to collect them yourself.

Pros

It saves a lot of work for your mother or chief bridesmaid.

Assuming the store is well chosen, your list will be easily accessible to most people in person, by telephone or via the internet.

There is no time delay and several people can have access to the list at one time and in several locations.

You can contact the company in person, by telephone or by e-mail for advice.

Cons

You will be restricted to choosing all your presents from one store and you do run the risk of your home looking like a smaller version of the store you chose your presents in.

Your guests will be restricted to one store, so you need to make sure there is one near to most guests, or that they are happy to use the telephone or internet.

Guests don't usually wrap their own gifts or give them to you in person.

A list with a specialised wedding gift list company

There are companies that specialise in running wedding gift lists, and you can benefit from their huge experience. As with a store list, you contact the company and register with it, then meet up with their staff in their offices or at your home to discuss your individual requirements, or talk with them on the phone. They will show you an extensive range of catalogues and a basic list, which you personalise with all the details of the gifts you would like. The company holds the list for you and keeps it up to date, sending you regular updates. Some companies charge for the service, others don't.

Guests contact the company by telephone or via the internet to view the list, make their choice and dictate the accompanying message. Generally, the gifts are available at normal retail prices, possibly with a small handling charge. The company keeps all the details until you have approved the list, then they order the goods and send them direct to you after the wedding. This system means that there is a delay before you receive your gifts, and the company will let you know the lead times (the length of time between the order being placed and the goods being dispatched by the supplier) involved.

Choosing Where to Have Your Wedding Gift List

Pros

It saves a lot of work for your mother or chief bridesmaid.

They are geared up to knowing what sort of presents most couples would like and normally offer a wider range of goods than most department stores.

They are generally more flexible than stores and some of them may allow you to include more unusual items – such as paintings or plants – on your list.

There is no geographical restriction as you can access the gifts from any location.

You can contact the company in person, by telephone or by e-mail for advice.

Cons

The companies tend to have offices rather than shops, so unless they have internet access your guests may not be able to see the presents they are buying.

Not everyone has access to the internet, especially some of your older guests, and not everyone is happy to make purchases online.

Some guests will prefer cash transactions rather than buying on credit or debit cards.

Guests may prefer to write their own message and deliver the gift in person.

There is a delay before you receive your wedding gifts; you should find out in advance what that will be.

A list with a number of different individual shops

For this option, you could create your own list, as with the first option, then group your gifts so one shop has a list of the tableware you would like, another has a list of the more decorative items such as lamps, cushions and vases, and so on until all your choices are placed with one store or another. The service is usually provided free of charge by the stores.

You inform your guests where the various lists are held and they visit the individual shops to make their purchases and take them away for wrapping and delivering.

Pros

It saves a lot of work for your mother or chief bridesmaid.

You can choose from a wide range of presents.

Guests will wrap their own gifts, write a personal message and deliver them.

Cons

This option can be quite frustrating for guests as they have to contact or visit several shops to find out what you are looking for. The temptation may just be to go for the first place on the list and choose something from there.

Guests who are not local may not be able to get to the shops.

A list held with an internet wedding gift list service

This is similar to the wedding gift company option, although entirely online. There are fewer choices and you need to be sure of the exact service they are offering. You contact them and register with them to personalise their basic list, and it is automatically kept up to date as people make purchases. It is usually free of charge.

Guests view the list online to make their choices and purchases, and write their messages. The company then makes one delivery about ten weeks after you have finalised the list (that is, gone through it and done any necessary swapping around), so there will be a delay before you receive your gifts.

Pros

It saves a lot of work for your mother or chief bridesmaid.

You can compile your list in the comfort of your own home.

Guests can choose and buy their gifts in the comfort of their own homes.

The system ensures that the list is always completely up to date.

Cons

Not everyone has access to the internet, especially some of your older guests, and not everyone is happy to make purchases online.

Some guests will prefer cash transactions rather than buying on credit or debit cards.

Many people like to ask the person organising the list for advice before they make their choice.

Guests may prefer to write their own message and deliver the gift in person.

There will be a delay before delivery of the gifts and usually only one delivery is made.

Choosing Where to Have Your Wedding Gift List

Making your decision

Your decision will depend on your own circumstances and those of your guests, so you need to think about the pros and cons of each option in relation to your friends and family. Try to make a choice that will suit most of the people most of the time! Here are the questions to ask that will help you make your choice.

- Does anyone have time to administer the list?
- Would your guests prefer to talk to you about the gifts or go to a store?
- Are most of your guests grouped locally or are they widely spread?
- Do you have access to the internet?
- Do your guests have access to the internet, and will they be happy to buy online?
- How much time do you have before the wedding?
- Would you prefer to write out your own list or customise an existing one?
- What kind of gifts are you likely to include?
- Would you like to know how the list is going on a regular basis?
- Would your guests prefer to have their gifts delivered direct to you or to wrap and give them to you personally?
- Do you need any gifts stored for you?
- Do you intend to organise a display of the wedding gifts?

Which company – which store?

If you have chosen a store or internet option, you'll need to decide which one you want to use. As with any choices involved in your wedding, it is a good idea to talk with two or three companies offering that particular service so that you can make an informed decision as to which is the best one for you.

There are number of basic factors you will want to compare and these are some of the points you might want to consider.

- What are the basic costs?
- Does the company offer a wide range of gifts of the kind you want?
- How many stores does it have and where are they located?
- Can the company be contacted by telephone?
- Can the company be contacted online?
- Is a service charge added for the guests?
- What are the payment options?
- What are the delivery options?
- What are the delivery charges?

You might also want to consider the added extras that make a service excellent rather than just good. Jot down some scores out of ten for each point when you contact the company and it should be easier to make your final decision.

Choosing Where to Have Your Wedding Gift List

- Are the staff pleasant to deal with?
- Did they return your calls and deal with things promptly and efficiently?
- Will they visit you at home to personalise your list?
- Is the company's website well designed and easy to navigate?
- Does it offer a gift-wrapping service?
- Does it have a storage service?
- Do you think your guests would be happy to deal with this company?

Chapter 3

Letting Your Guests Know You Have a Wedding Gift List

It's no good going to all the effort of compiling a wedding gift list, then keeping your well-planned list to yourself. You need to tell your guests what you have organised and how they can access the list. If you don't, they may not realise there is a list at all, or they may be too embarrassed to ask, in which case they will go out a buy whatever they think you would like. One couple I know, Sarah and David, put together a very thorough list but were less organised about publicising it. They received three wrought iron vegetable stands with wicker baskets, 84 whisky tumblers and more crystal bowls than anyone could break in a lifetime! You have been warned...

A note with your invitations

The easiest way of letting your guests know that you have compiled a wedding gift list is to put a note in with your invitations explaining where your list is held and how they can use it.

Letting Your Guests Know You Have a Wedding Gift List

If you feel it is a bit presumptuous to put such a note in with your invitations, go back to Chapter 1 and remind yourself of the good reasons why you decided to create a wedding list in the first place. If you are happy with the list principle, this really is the best way to let people know about it. Otherwise, you have to contact them again when you have received their acceptance to tell them about the list, which will probably feel far more awkward, or you are putting the onus on them to contact you to ask you what you would like.

You can add a line or two on the bottom of your instructions on how to get to the ceremony venue, or from the ceremony to the reception, for example, or you could print a separate card or note that your guests can slip into a pocket or handbag to keep the details handy for when they are out shopping or using their computer at home or at work.

Most PCs have a business card wizard option that is ideal for creating your own cards, with all the contact details, that can be put in with your invitations. Some wedding gift list services have their own cards, which they can give you to use in the same way.

Your card or note does not have to be a massive notice screaming 'Buy us a present', but equally you should not assume everyone knows you have a wedding list, or that they will know how to access or use one. Even if your list is being administered by your parents, do let the guests know it is available and provide them with a contact telephone number so that they can get in touch easily to find out the sort of presents you might like.

What to say

A short note providing all the details of your wedding list arrangements will be quite sufficient. For example:

- Should you wish to use our wedding gift list, please ring Marjorie Smith on 01256 678907 and she will be pleased to send you a copy.
- Should you wish to use our wedding gift list, you will find it at the Wedding Services desk on the ground floor in Smith's Department Store, High Street, Anytown.
- Should you wish to use it, our wedding gift list is held by Wedding Lists. You can telephone them on 020 6765 5678 or access the list online at www.weddinglist.co.uk.

If they do not want to use the wedding list, your guests can simply ignore this information, but you will probably find that most will want to consult the list so they can be sure their gift is something you have chosen yourself.

Chapter 4
Keeping Your List Up to Date

However you decide to operate your wedding list, it is crucial to keep it up to date, otherwise it defeats the object of having one in the first place.

Another advantage of keeping abreast of what people are buying is that you may be able to influence your guests' choices. If everyone is choosing to buy items of crockery, for example, you could talk to the person administering the list and ask him or her to guide people towards other items. It is one of the skills of someone experienced in the wedding gift field to influence guests towards your highest priority items, perhaps simply by saying something like: 'Quite a few guests have already chosen to buy china and I know from talking with Mary that she is really hoping to receive some bed linen or towels. Perhaps that might be a good choice?'

Since you will almost certainly also have to get some items for your home yourself, you will also get a better idea of things you will need to buy if you are in touch with what remains on the list.

A personal list

If the list is with you or your mother, then you need to stay vigilant and organised. You should always know exactly who has copies of the list, make sure they have instructions to let you know what they have chosen, and give them a date by which to contact you. If they miss the date, you'll need to give them a ring to explain that someone else needs to look at the list and could they kindly let you know what they have chosen. If they won't be hurried, politely ask them if they wouldn't mind calling you when they have made their choice to check that the item is still on the list. Then you can continue to circulate the list to your other guests and the first guest will have to take the risk that someone else will get in first with their choice.

A store or wedding list company list

If your list is with a store, wedding list or internet company, find out the standard arrangements for keeping you up to date. It is most likely that you will be e-mailed on a weekly basis to let you know which gifts have already been chosen, the name and address of the person who purchased the present, and the message he or she put with the present if it is being delivered directly to you.

Keeping Your List Up to Date

Making changes

If you have your own list, you can easily add items you may have forgotten at the beginning, and most wedding list companies will also be quite happy for you to add extra things to the list if you had forgotten them. After all, their job is to ensure that you receive the presents you most want.

In either case, you should also remember to remove items from the list if you receive them from people who have chosen not to use your list.

Keeping notes

Another advantage of an up-to-date list is that you will have a complete record of who is buying what that you can use to start your thank-you letters in good time. Tick them off when they have been written and sent off so you don't miss anybody out, write to the same person twice, or thank the right person for the wrong gift!

Chapter 5
Thank-you Letters

When people have given you a generous and thoughtful gift, it is only common courtesy to send them a thank-you letter, even if you thanked them in person when you received the gift. It is particularly important to thank them properly if they have not actually handled a gift but it has been sent direct from the wedding gift company, otherwise they may think it was never received.

Letter, card or e-mail?
It may seem old-fashioned, but a hand-written note is definitely the most polite and appreciated way to thank those who gave you wedding gifts. It doesn't have to be very long – just a few words of thanks for the gift, saying how useful it will be or attractive it is, and a line or two about the wedding day or honeymoon will do nicely.

The task is not nearly so daunting if you organise yourself so that you keep your list of the givers' names and addresses, the writing paper, envelopes and stamps in one place easily to hand, rather than having to gather together everything you need each time you sit down to write a letter or two. You could buy

Thank-you Letters

appropriately decorated wedding stationery off the shelf, or order some specially printed paper with your other wedding stationery (invitations, order of service, etc.); these are ideal for thank you letters.

If you really can't face hand-writing all those letters, another possibility is to type them on your PC but I feel this option is definitely a poor second best. People do know how easy it is to send the same or a very similar letter to everyone. Where the PC does come into its own is that you can use your list of thank-you letters to start a database of addresses for next year's Christmas cards.

You can also buy printed thank-you cards on which you fill in the present on a dotted line and sign the bottom. I have to say I'm no great fan of these, but I will grudgingly admit that they could just pass in some circumstances, perhaps in thanks for a wedding gift that was bought from a collection of work colleagues whom the bride doesn't know particularly well. Exercise your judgement if you decide to use these at all.

Younger guests might be quite happy to receive an e-mail acknowledgement and this is a good way of writing if you have a lot to say and it doesn't have to be formal in style. Older guests are very unlikely to find e-mail acceptable. Again, use your judgement.

Thank-you Letters

Getting ahead

If you are fully up to speed with what has been bought and by whom, you can make a start on your thank-you letters before your wedding. It may seem slightly strange to write before the wedding but when you come back from honeymoon and return to work, the last thing you are going to want to do in the evenings is sit down and plough your way through a long list of letters. On the other hand, writing a few letters at a time in advance is quite enjoyable, you can make them much more personal, and you will be pleased you did so. You will then have fewer to write when you are home again after your honeymoon.

Another way of tackling your thank-you letters is to make a start on each letter before you go away and then just add one final paragraph about the wedding day or the honeymoon when you get home. Make sure you have an adequate supply of the same type of pen – a jumble of different inks would look very shoddy!

Read the messages

Do make sure that you relate the right gift to the right people and read the messages on the gift list or the gift itself before you write your thank-you letters. It may sound like a very obvious point, but it's possible to get confused when you receive a lot of gifts or you are working from a store list.

For example, your mother's four sisters might have decided to club together to give you a joint gift. If one of them purchased the gift, it would be recorded with the wedding list company as coming only from, say, 'Mrs Alice Evans'. The message with the gift, however, would tell you that the present is actually from: 'Alice and Edward, Mary and David, Janet and John, and Sally and Peter', which gives you a quite different list of letters to write.

Groups of friends also frequently club together to buy one large gift rather than a collection of smaller individual items, so you will need to know that ten friends decided you'd love the gas barbecue for £350, instead of ten less exciting (to them) individual presents, such as chopping boards, milk pans or bed linen for £35 each.

Keeping in contact

It is also a good idea to use your thank-you letters to make sure everyone has your address, telephone and mobile numbers, and e-mail address – especially, of course, if you are moving house when you marry. You can easily print some labels or slips on your PC and place them on or in your letter.

Chapter 6

How to Plan Your Wedding Gift List

Your wedding presents should be looked on as a solid starting block on which you can stamp your own style over the years. Obviously, no two lists are identical and it is up to you to create a list that really represents what you would most like to receive. That requires some serious thought to ensure that you and your fiancé are entirely happy to live with the items on your list for a long time.

To help you do that, I have given plenty of guidance on the important points to consider, plus all the information you need on how to actually go about it. Detailed information on the categories of items are listed in the next chapter, then in Chapter 12 there's a complete list for you to fill in, with some spaces for you to write in any additions (perhaps you and your fiancé just can't call a house a home if it doesn't have a samovar, a wallpapering table or a couple of nesting boxes for the garden). If you use this 'memory jogger', you'll end up with a fairly comprehensive list of items you would like to include on your wedding gift list.

How to Plan Your Wedding Gift List

To start with, it is a good idea to follow a step-by-step sequence when compiling your list to avoid leaving anything out. I'll go into more detail on each point on the following pages.

- Think about what kind of items you need, depending on your own circumstances.
- Decide roughly how long your list should be. You should include enough items to allow your guests a good choice, but not so many that the list looks intimidating or greedy.
- Have a good range of prices, and think about a sensible limit.
- Run through the complete list and cross off everything you already have or are being given either new or second hand. Go through again and cross out anything that you really do not want to receive.
- Go through the following chapter and think about how the categories of gift relate to the items you are likely to choose.
- Add unusual items that relate to you specifically. Perhaps you would like to ask for some skiing equipment or a pair of binoculars!
- Now prioritise your list, marking which items you really want and which are less important.
- Finally add the detail of colours, patterns or brands you would like and do a final check for the length and price range of the list.

How to Plan Your Wedding Gift List

What to put on your list

There are various factors that will influence what you put on your wedding gift list. If you have lived at home until the time of your wedding and are moving into a new flat or house, your list is likely to be very much focused on the home as you will need things like furniture, linen, electrical goods and kitchen items such as a toaster, a kettle, saucepans, china, cutlery and so on.

If, though, you are combining two flats into one you may already have one – if not two – of many of the basics such as kettles and toasters. What you may not have is anything smart or anything you have actually chosen yourselves. In this instance, your list may well comprise a smart dinner service, glasses, cutlery, better kitchen equipment, linen and some stylish individual items such as lamps and cushions.

At the other extreme, you may already live in an established home and have most of the household items you need. If you are in this fortunate position you may wish to consider including things such as wine, charitable donations, garden furniture or plants on your list.

Another factor is that everyone has a slightly different idea about what they do and do not consider as a suitable wedding present. One couple might refuse to put mugs on the list – or a guest avoid choosing them – because the very word conjurers up images of a cupboard full of garage give-aways and freebies from Easter eggs or business exhibitions. On the other hand, another guest may snap up your mugs because they know how much you both enjoy your tea.

If you are planning your list with a view to filling your home and never buying anything else, that's fine. But if you like change and variety, you don't have to choose, say, an expensive set of cutlery that you are then stuck with. Lifestyles vary so much now and only you can really know what you will and won't make good use of in your married life.

How long is a list?

You should know roughly how many guests will potentially be looking at your list so you can make sure you have enough items on the list for everyone – and allow plenty of choice. As a general rule of thumb it is best to put down absolutely everything you would like. Being contacted by the person who is running your list two weeks before the wedding and being asked to think of more presents you would like is not a good situation. It leads to panic decisions, which are very much against the spirit of the occasion, and you will almost certainly add things that you don't really want. It is far better to go a bit over the top to start with so you have a good range of items.

Including plenty of gifts also means that your guests have plenty of choice, so there will be no problems for the latecomers who otherwise might find there is nothing available in their budget range.

Having done this, however, you may feel that your list is much too long in relation to the number of guests. In that case, it may be worth making a back-up list of items that have a fairly low priority rather than publishing your entire list right from the start. You can then fall back on this list if necessary. If you do include absolutely everything, wedding guests quite often think along the lines of, 'I know it's a low priority but I'm going to give them the cockerel doorstop because I'm not buying anything that is part of a set or anything breakable'. If this item hadn't been on the list the same guest would probably have been quite happy to buy the cream jug to go with your dinner service!

How much will guests have to spend?

You should bear in mind while you are working on your list that you need to offer your guests plenty of choice at the right prices. So try to ensure that you have a good spread of prices. As I said, the average spend is £83, but that means that some guests will spend more (especially parents and close older relatives) and a great many will spend less. You may have friends who would like to buy more reasonably priced gifts, families who want their children to give you their own present, or family members who are happy to club together to buy one larger item.

Generally speaking, if you are putting china, glass and cutlery on your list you will automatically have a good spread of prices, which allows for the guest who gives you a pair of wine glasses and another who gives you a decanter and 12 whisky tumblers. Try to choose presents that you feel are sensibly priced. It is quite normal for a fine bone china dinner plate with a patterned border to cost somewhere in the region of £30 but some are much more expensive and some are less so.

Start crossing off

Now you have a picture in your mind of the sort of things you need, cross off anything you already have, though, if they are old or bargain-basement items that you would like to replace, by all means leave them on the list. At the prioritising stage, you may want to make them a lower priority than the things you really need.

There are also bound to be items you know you wouldn't use in a million years. Things like fondue sets or bread makers might be top of some people's lists but are sure to be right down the bottom of others.

The basic list

Now to the real planning. Look at the detailed text in the next chapter that identifies things you should be thinking about when you finalise and prioritise your list. For example, is it better to ask for the best quality towels or would it be more sensible to go for something cheaper for now and replace them when you re-do your bathroom in a couple of years?

Add to the list

You can also add those items that are really unique to you, which no one else would think about including on a wedding list.

Prioritise your list

The next stage is to prioritise your list by indicating which items you would like most of all and which items it would be nice to have but are certainly not as important. This is easy to do if your mother is running the list, but most wedding gift list providers allow you to specify which items you place higher importance on getting than others.

Make the final section

Finally, go into the real detail of what you would like, including colours, patterns, quality and brands. You will know what you do and don't like and should follow your own minds.

Having said that, it is sensible to think a little ahead. Do you have plans to move from the town to the country (or vice versa), before long? Are you both going to stay in the same field of work for the foreseeable future? Will you be following the same hobbies and sports? These are the sort of factors that could turn what seems a sensible choice now into a big mistake later on.

To begin with there might be just the two of you in a tiny flat with an undersized kitchen so you've specified a small-capacity bread maker. Even if you have no thoughts of starting a family just yet, you will be having friends and family for supper and, for an extra bit of worktop space, everyone can have enough of your home-baked bread. If you know that you will change to a king-sized bed as soon as space allows, what will become of your beautiful 100 per cent linen duvet cover and pillow cases that fit your current conventional double? A round-bottomed wok is not going to be any use at all when you upgrade from your present gas cooker to the ceramic hob you yearn for.

Perhaps you admire a current interior decoration trend – plain, minimalist design or flowery flounces, for instance – and think this is a good opportunity to create these magazine surroundings. But is it really *your* style? Will it be your style in a couple of years? You might have to restrict your bathroom décor for years to come because of your half-dozen very good quality and indestructable towels in the must-have colour at the time of your wedding. Fashions soon change and become hard to live with.

Chapter 7
Choosing Your Wedding Presents

This chapter looks at the various factors involved in choosing items for your wedding gift list under headings such as kitchenware, electrical goods and china. I haven't covered every item you are likely to put on your list but just the considerations that may help you in your choices.

It is a good idea to do your research before writing down what you would like. Go round the shops, look at retail catalogues, visit websites and find out what's out there. Chances are you haven't spent a lot of time looking at saucepans before now, but a few hours invested now will really be worth it! Magazines are a great source of inspiration, ideas and information, too, so abandon *Hello!* or *Vogue* for a while in favour of *Good Housekeeping* or *BBC Homes*. Check out the latest *Which?* reports, too, as they will focus your mind on the most useful features of each item. At the time of writing, you can access *Which? Online* for £7.75 a month and it might be worth subscribing now, even if you don't keep it going for long.

Don't be disappointed if no one buys your really practical items. Put yourselves in your guests' shoes; it might be that they just don't see them as suitable wedding presents. Put these items on your list but be prepared to use wedding present money or your own money to buy them when your list is being finalised.

Remember, some shops and wedding gift list companies will give you 10 per cent discount on items you purchase yourselves when your list is being finalised so this is a good time to buy items you know you are going to need at some stage.

Kitchenware

Depending on how much of a foodie you are, you may already have a fairly well-equipped kitchen. Or you might be looking at your wedding gift list as the perfect opportunity to upgrade to better-quality kitchenware than you already have that should, hopefully, last you throughout your married life.

When choosing your presents make sure you look at manufacturers' guarantees; they are there for a reason. Stainless steel with a lifetime guarantee will last for ever and is worth paying for. Cast iron or non-stick items with a ten-year guarantee will only last that long or even longer if they are looked after carefully.

Saucepans

A good set of saucepans is essential to most kitchens. Most people have their own opinions on what sort of pan they like

Choosing Your Wedding Presents

best. Make up your own mind, and once you have decided you should opt for the best quality in that material that you feel happy to put on your list. The main options are stainless steel, enamel, copper or those with a non-stick surface. Cheap aluminium pans are pretty much a waste of money; they don't last long and, because they are so thin, food tends to burn very easily.

Personally I like stainless steel. It can be scrubbed clean if anything gets burnt on to it and, if looked after, will last a lifetime.

Copper is very expensive and difficult to keep clean. You need to be quite certain it is what you want before opting for it.

Enamel saucepans can be very heavy and most of them come with a pouring lip rather than a completely circular rim. Although this may seem all right it can be very annoying not being able to make a tight seal on a saucepan when cooking vegetables.

Non-stick saucepans will probably have a shorter life expectancy than other ranges, although they may be cheaper.

With both enamel and non-stick pans it is very important to remember that you should never use metal cooking utensils as they will scratch enamel and will 'tear' the non-stick coating on your pans. If used on a gas hob, you will have to watch the height of your flame carefully. If constantly used on a ring that is set too high the wooden handles on enamel pans will char and the plastic or phenolonic handles on non-stick pans will melt.

Take into account the weight of the pans. With stainless steel, the heavier the better but some cast iron pans are so heavy that they are just a menace. If you can't lift the empty pan, it will be seriously unsafe when filled with boiling liquid.

Most companies offer a basic starter set of saucepans that will probably comprise a milk pan, 16 cm (6 in), 18 cm (7 in) and 20 cm (8 in) saucepans and a frying pan (skillet).

A useful addition to most sets of saucepans is a steamer insert. Steamers are great for cooking vegetables such as broccoli or cauliflower over another saucepan. Not only do you save on hob space, but your vegetables retain their flavour and nutritional value much better than when they are boiled.

In addition to these items you may want to consider a 22 cm (8½ in) saucepan, a covered sauté pan and a large frying pan. If you are a keen cook, think about other, more specialist pans such as a double boiler or a wok.

Casserole dishes and oven-to-table ware

Casserole dishes (Dutch ovens) can be earthenware, porcelain or cast iron. A couple of Pyrex casseroles are also useful but don't make stunning presents, so are something you might like to buy for yourself.

I am a complete cast iron fan. Although they are heavy they are fantastic to cook with because they can be used both on the hob and in the oven and can be used at high temperatures. That means you can brown your onions, meat and so on in the casserole on the hob, then pop on the lid and put it in the oven. If you have earthenware casseroles, you have to start off in a frying pan, then transfer everything to your casserole. If you don't mind washing up this is fine.

A good combination of casseroles would be 20 cm (8 in), 24 cm (9½ in) and 28 cm (11 in). A 20 cm (8 in) casserole is the perfect size for making supper for a family of four – I must use mine just about every day. A 28 cm (11 in) is the size you would use for making coq au vin or boeuf bourgignon for a dinner party. The 24 cm (9½ in) is just a useful in-between size.

If you are cooking for a lot of people, these larger casseroles are also perfect for cooking pasta, potatoes and rice.

For baking dishes, the choice is basically earthenware, porcelain or cast iron. There is a huge range of makes, quality, colours and prices to chose from.

Cast iron oven-to-table ware is not so readily available as the other options. Both it and enamel tend to be difficult to clean once something such as lasagne has baked on for an hour or so.

Rectangular baking dishes are perfect for making all sorts of things from gratin dauphinoise to lasagne or apple crumble. A 26 cm (10 in) rectangular dish is just the right size to make lasagne for six people. A 32 cm (13 in) one will feed eight to ten. A smaller one is good for serving two.

Ramekins (custard cups) are really useful oven-to-table items and a great addition to most sets of china. They can be

Choosing Your Wedding Presents

used for starters such as baked eggs, for puddings like crème brûlée, and as sauce dishes if you don't like having jars on the table. Mine were seriously overused when my children were small (I used to give them a few sweets (candies) in a ramekin after a meal!).

Kitchen china

You can buy some lovely inexpensive everyday china but do find out whether or not the one you choose is likely to be discontinued if it is something you plan to keep for years or to add to after the wedding. The main tableware manufacturers will normally give you a guarantee that a certain pattern will run for at least the next five years but, if this is not the case, err on the side of caution and go for more than you think you need.

Everyday plates quite often end up sitting in the dishwasher, or in the fridge with food, leftovers and cake on. It is very annoying if you're about to serve up supper to go to the cupboard and find you have run out of plates. For the sake of a few extra pounds it is worth buying additional plates. I now have 16 place settings of the china my family uses most of the time – and we need them!

I always think that 12 is a good starting point but you know your own lifestyle and the decision is ultimately yours. Perhaps it is worth looking in your parents' cupboards and seeing what numbers they have.

You should certainly steer clear of boxed sets of china. If

Choosing Your Wedding Presents

you buy an 18-piece boxed set – six dinner plates, six side plates and six oatmeal bowls – and one item gets broken you will have to buy another 18-piece set just to be able to replace one item (assuming the range is still available).

When deciding what to go for in everyday china you are obviously going to want dinner plates. In addition you will need side plates and oatmeal bowls. If you are likely to use your everyday china for entertaining you may also want to consider adding dessert/salad plates and soup plates.

Another item that has become very popular over the past few years is the pasta plate. Pasta is very popular now and a big, deep plate is the perfect thing to eat it from. Do, however, bear in mind that these large plates may not fit in your dishwasher and what started out as a quick and easy pasta supper won't seem so quick and easy if you have to wash up by hand.

As far as cups are concerned, very few of us use teacups and saucers every day and it's probably most practical to go for mugs in everyday china, which can be used for tea or coffee. Sometimes it's nice to have a great big breakfast cup and saucer full of tea on a Sunday morning but generally speaking we all seem to live our lives so fast that a mug will be far more useful and take up less room in the dishwasher.

One set of china for all occasions

More and more couples feel that using up a large proportion of the value of their wedding gift list on a formal dinner service that may get used only once a year or so is just not worth it. With the huge expansion of the 'casual dining' market, more and more companies make china that is suitable for using all the time.

These ranges are fairly all-encompassing and most companies include matching lasagne dishes, salad bowls, ramekins (custard cups), etc., which don't necessarily come with smart dinner services or with cheaper china ranges.

There is currently a lot of plain white china on the market, in fine bone china and in porcelain, with prices varying according to quality. White china can look stunning when 'dressed up' for a dinner party but it is also eminently practical for everyday use.

Kitchen knives

A set of good-quality kitchen knives is another item worth investing in. It is said that a good chef would give up anything rather than his or her favourite knives. There are hundreds of kitchen knives on the market but, again, look at the guarantees and go for the best quality you can. I was making a casserole one day and had used a fairly poor quality knife to chop up the meat. As I was washing up I noticed that a small chunk of metal had come out of the middle of the blade. I couldn't risk feeding my children metal so the whole casserole went in the bin, as did the knife!

Good-quality knives are quite expensive and should never be put in the dishwasher. They come in a range of styles and it

Choosing Your Wedding Presents

is, obviously, a matter of personal choice what you go for. The two main materials used for the blades of kitchen knives are stainless steel and carbon steel, with the vast majority being stainless steel.

As far as style is concerned, knives tend to be one long piece of metal (such as Global knives), or have a rivetted handle (such as Sabatier) or have a solid handle of a completely different material from the blade.

A standard set of knives might comprise a 10 cm (4 in) paring knife, a 13 cm (5 in) utility knife (with a serrated blade), a 20 cm (8 in) cook's knife, a carving knife and a bread knife (which you'll need unless you only ever buy sliced bread!). To this you may also wish to add a carving fork and a sharpening steel. Alternatively you may prefer to have a three-piece carving set to match your cutlery.

If you do decide to go for a knife block set – a set of knives and the block to hold them – it might be worth asking the store or wedding gift list company if they can be put on your list as individual items rather than as one large present. A good set of kitchen knives in a wooden block can cost hundreds of pounds; someone might opt to buy the whole set but if this doesn't happen they might still be being sold if priced separately.

Keeping sharp knives in a drawer with a lot of other kitchen utensils can be very dangerous. Most companies have the blocks specifically designed to hold their knives but if you are short of

Choosing Your Wedding Presents

space on your kitchen worktop a wall mounted magnetic knife rack is an alternative that is well worth considering.

If you have included a knife block set or a carving set on your list you might well find that a sharpening steel is already included. Knife sharpeners are a matter of personal choice: the main types are a traditional sharpening steel, which is a long rod you run the blade of the knife along, and a knife sharpener that you put on your kitchen work top and run the blade of the knife through.

Condiments

We all seem to eat so much salad nowadays and some of us are happy to make our dressing in a jug. If you prefer to let people mix their own dressing, separate bottles for your oil and vinegar that you put on the table make a great wedding present. These bottles come in all shapes and sizes. You can either go for two separate bottles or you may prefer to go for a combination pourer which holds both and has two pouring spouts.

Salt and pepper mills also make great and useful gifts.

Baking equipment

If you enjoy baking, you'll want to include some basic cookware on your list, but if you've never made a cake in your life – and don't anticipate doing so – don't fill up your cupboards with equipment you are never going to use. A clean smooth glass bottle makes a great rolling pin anyway!

Choosing Your Wedding Presents

If you do include these items on your list, again it is worth going for the best quality as they will last longer and give better service.

Other kitchen items

A lot of smaller or less expensive kitchen items are things that you simply have to go into a shop and choose. What is available will depend on current trends and you will also be guided by what you feel is a reasonable price to pay for a particular item.

If you take a bread bin, for example, you can find perfectly functional wooden, enamel or stainless steel ones for around £20. You can also, at the other end of the spectrum, find hugely expensive 'designer label' ones. You will know what you like and what you are happy putting on your list.

Electrical goods

Electrical items change on a regular basis as manufacturers struggle to keep up with our changing tastes in kitchen design. One year everything is navy blue or green, the next year it is chrome and the year after that it is matt stainless steel. My mother still has the kettle she had when I was a child, whereas today kettles, toasters and other small items seem to have become entirely disposable goods that can be changed on a whim.

You have to choose whether you are going to ask for traditional items that will last, and so spend time researching the most cost-effective, efficient and high-quality models, or if you prefer things that will do a sound job and be replaced after a couple of years. Personally I would rather go for good-quality items that will last rather than have to buy new ones every 18 months, which in the long run is a false economy.

A safe option is to stick with white or chrome, which is an especially good idea if you are going for the best quality as it will look good even if you change your colour scheme.

The best advice I can give you if you are looking for help with what to go for is to ask the staff in an electrical shop or the electrical department of a big department store. If nothing else, they will be able to tell you what the most popular models are at the time, which are the best quality, and so on.

Food processors

The best-known brands of food maker are probably Magimix, Kenwood and KitchenAid and spares for their models should be readily available. If you are going to have a food processor at all, it is worth investing in a quality model.

Kettles

Kettles come in all shapes and sizes and the best thing is to go for the best quality one you feel you can put on your list. Most are now cordless and with a window so you can see how much water is in it. If you are left handed and your partner is right handed, or vice versa, make sure you choose a kettle on a round base that can be put down facing any direction.

Choosing Your Wedding Presents

Microwave ovens

We all lead such busy lives nowadays that most kitchens are incomplete without a microwave even if it is just used for defrosting bread or reheating cold cups of coffee. There is an enormous range of microwaves on the market from the straightforward to the combination microwave/grill or microwave/convection oven and used well they can save enormous amounts of time and energy.

Think about what you are likely to use the oven for, how often, and how much space you have in the kitchen and decide accordingly on what type to buy. If you will only use it for basic things now and then, a cheaper model may be the right one for you.

Toasters

Probably the best toasters on the market are Dualit. They are fairly expensive, with the recommended retail price for a four-slice stainless steel toaster being around £170, but they do last for years. The thing that sets Dualit toasters apart from the rest is the fact that most others have a spring inside them to make the toast pop up once it is done. It is normally this spring that gives up the ghost and forces people to throw out their toaster and buy a replacement. Dualit toasters have a lever that lowers and raises the slices, which is very unlikely to break so your toaster should go on for years.

White goods

White goods are not a popular choice for guests when they look at wedding gift lists. With the possible exception of microwaves, they are fairly expensive and not everyone's idea of a perfect wedding present. The life expectancy of a washing machine could now be as little as 18 months and most people looking to spend a few hundred pounds on a wedding present will want to choose something longer lasting. However, you'll probably think most of them are essential, so you can either buy them for yourself or try to convince some of your generous relatives on the grounds of how important these items are.

It is worth doing your research on the various programmes they offer and their price, quality, reliability and guarantees. Consult *Which?* magazine, or access it online if you can, to find the ideal model for your pocket and lifestyle. Also, if you or your parents use a local domestic appliance repair man, it's well worth asking his advice. He will know which models are reliable and, more to the point, which are constantly needing repairs.

China

The first thing to consider with china is whether you are looking for a smart dinner service or one set of china that can be used for all occasions. The choice of china available now is enormous but there are a number of things that are worth taking into account.

Choosing Your Wedding Presents

Price
The price of dinner services varies enormously depending on quality and design. Although in the first instance you should choose your china depending on what you like, do bear in mind that guests may not like to buy very expensive dinner-service items. A guest who wishes to spend £100 is unlikely to be happy buying two soup plates. What's more, you need to be really sure you are going to want this same china for life if you pay that kind of money.

If you do find a china that you like but feel it is too expensive, ask your wedding gift list adviser to see what there is in a similar style, or look around yourself for something more appropriate. You may well find something you like even more at a fraction of the cost.

Pattern
There are some fantastic patterns around nowadays but, if you can't make up your mind what to go for, why not choose something simple that can be dressed up or down depending on your mood and the occasion? You can't go far wrong with plain white: it displays food well, is absolutely classic and timeless, and goes with everything so you can choose the brightest table linen and accessories. Alternatively you could choose a classic dinner service with a cobalt blue band, which looks beautiful on a table with cut crystal, white napkins and so on. However, if you replace the cut crystal and white linen with bright red funky

Choosing Your Wedding Presents

wine goblets, bright red napkins and bold flowers, none of which are hugely expensive, the whole table is lifted and looks much more contemporary. And you will still have a dinner service that you are going to be happy with in many years' time.

Generally speaking you will find that your smart china will be fine bone china or porcelain. Most of the traditional English tableware companies make fine bone china: French companies tend to make porcelain. As a rule, fine bone china is a slightly brighter white than porcelain.

> **Sophie and Alan**
>
> This couple fell in love with a beautiful Aynsley dinner service when they were getting married. They put it on their wedding gift list but no one gave them any of the pieces – hardly surprising when you consider that at the time a dinner plate was £67. They then decided to use some of their wedding present money to buy two place settings of the china and agreed that they would buy one more place setting on their wedding anniversary each year. This would mean that on their 10th wedding anniversary they would finally be up to 12 place settings.
>
> The years passed, they had children, bought a bigger house, supported the children through university. They have now been married for 22 years and still have only the two place settings, which are proudly displayed in a china cabinet.

Choosing Your Wedding Presents

Quantities

When deciding what quantities to go for in china, glass and cutlery always think big. When you have visitors it is amazing how much of everything you will get through in a day. Imagine Sunday lunch when your parents come over, or when you have children in a few years' time. What about when your siblings visit with *their* children or it's your turn to host Christmas? You may have wondered when you first got married and there was just the two of you why you decided to ask for so much of these items, but later on you'll be pleased you did.

As a rule of thumb it is usually sensible to go for at least two more place settings than you imagine you will need, and most people find that going for six of anything is simply not enough in the long term. Eight should be your minimum.

What to buy

Spend a bit of time imagining yourselves using your dinner service so you can work out exactly what pieces you would like to have. You will know yourselves the sort of food you are likely to serve.

For a dinner party you will probably use:

Starter/soup: salad/dessert plate or soup plate plus a side plate for bread
Main course: dinner plate
Pudding: oatmeal bowl (or dessert plate)
Cheese: side plate
Coffee/tea: coffee/teacup

As I have already mentioned, pasta seems to have become one of the mainstays of our diet and you may want to add pasta plates to the fine china on your wedding gift list. If you do, think carefully about how many to go for. If you have decided to go for 12 place settings of the other china, consider asking for only eight pasta plates. They are fairly expensive (normally more so than a dinner plate) and in reality if you are using your best china for a dinner party are you likely to serve pasta as a main course?

Place settings
These are the constituents of a full place setting:

- Dinner plate
- Salad/dessert plate
- Side plate
- Soup plate
- Oatmeal bowl
- Coffee cup and saucer
- Teacup and saucer

Dinner plates are usually 27 cm (10 in) in diameter. Some manufacturers now make dinner plates as large as 28–32 cm (11–13 in), which are very popular and food looks lovely presented on them. But do remember to check that they will fit in your dishwasher or they could turn out to be a big nuisance

Choosing Your Wedding Presents

when you're clearing up after a large dinner party. If you are serving several courses you don't need huge portions of anything and your food could well end up looking lost on an enormous plate unless you have time to perform restaurant-style presentation!

If you like serving your pudding on a plate, consider not having oatmeal bowls and going for double quantities of salad/dessert plates.

Opting for both coffee cups and teacups can prove to be a very expensive option. Many manufacturers now offer one straight-sided cup that can be used for both. These are normally called palladian teacups.

Serving pieces

Serving pieces for formal china tend to be fairly expensive and it is worth giving careful consideration to what you include on your wedding gift list.

The items I use most are my oval platters, which I might put starters such as smoked salmon on, and my creamer and sugar bowl, which we use with coffee. If I am having a dinner party I usually put butter in four ramekins (custard cups) and space them around the table rather than having just one butter dish that someone is always waiting for.

Of all serving pieces, the least used ones have to be the soup tureen and the coffee pot. If you have friends over to supper would you really bother trying to heat a cumbersome tureen,

Choosing Your Wedding Presents

decanting your soup from a saucepan into it and then taking it to the table? In reality most of us would serve the soup into bowls in the kitchen and then bring them to the table on a tray. Likewise with a coffee pot; nowadays most people make coffee in a cafetière and take it to the table. Both of the above are expensive and probably doomed to live in a cupboard collecting dust.

Glassware

I have been to dinner parties for 12 where we have each had a separate glass for pre-dinner drinks, red wine, white wine, water and liqueurs. That made 60 glasses to wash up! Fortunately a lot of people are happy to drink wine – or whatever – all evening and out of the same glass. You need to think about what kind of glasses you want, the quality, the style, the numbers and the priority you place on them on your wedding list. It's very much up to you and your lifestyle.

The biggest decision to make when choosing glassware is whether or not you are happy to wash your glasses by hand. You can't beat drinking a really good wine out of stylish crystal wine glasses but they should never be put in the dishwasher so you could be left with a serious amount of washing up after entertaining.

Hand-cut crystal, such as Waterford, Stuart Crystal or Edinburgh Crystal, tends to be fairly expensive and so does heavier lead content uncut or etched crystal, such as William Yeoward.

Choosing Your Wedding Presents

The more traditional crystal companies often call their glasses wine, large wine and goblet. Traditionally these would have been used for white wine, red wine and water. In addition to the wine glasses, most ranges include a champagne flute, a tumbler and a highball glass, and some ranges also have brandy, sherry, port and liqueur glasses. Both the Dartington Wine Master and Riedel Vinum ranges of smart, classic-shaped, crystal offer a complete choice of lovely fine crystal glasses from liqueur and port right through to enormous red wine glasses. More contemporary ranges might offer only offer wine and large wine, champagne flute, tumbler and highball.

If you would prefer glasses that will go in the dishwasher you will have to go for glass not crystal. If this is the case err on the side of caution. Glass is considerably cheaper than crystal so go for larger quantities to have a few spares and accept that there will be breakages.

If you want champagne glasses, there are three main types: traditional flutes, champagne saucers or hollow stem flutes. Hollow stem flutes are rather difficult to clean if they have been used for buck's fizz or kir royale as it is virtually impossible to get even a baby's bottle brush right to the bottom of the glass.

If you are beer drinkers you may also want to consider some beer glasses. Again the range is large and your initial choice will be whether you would prefer to have traditional tankards or taller, straighter glasses.

Cutlery

Cutlery can be expensive and account for a large chunk of a wedding gift list so it is important that you give it careful consideration. The three main choices in cutlery are stainless steel, silver plate or sterling silver and again everyone has their own ideas about what they do and don't like.

As with china, go for the best quality you can reasonably expect your guests to buy. Check that the design you choose is not likely to be discontinued, if you think you may want to add to it later.

Stainless steel is the most practical option because it is completely dishwasher safe and a good quality set will last for ever.

Silver plate comes in various qualities and the price varies accordingly. Most silver plate is dishwasher proof but should not be put in the same compartment as stainless steel.

Sterling silver is very expensive, with a table fork or dessert spoon costing about £60 each and a table knife about £40. The reason for the difference in price is that all knives have a stainless steel blade and a hollow, weighted handle whereas a fork or spoon is one solid piece of silver.

The sort of place setting that you decide to go for will depend on what you envisage using your cutlery for. If it is only for everyday use you may feel that you just need table forks and knives, dessert spoons and teaspoons. If you are going to use it for entertaining, work out what you will need by imagining the sort of menu you would normally go for.

A standard seven-piece place setting is designed to be used as follows:

Soup: soup spoon
Main course: table knife and table fork
Pudding: dessert spoon and dessert fork
Cheese: dessert knife
Coffee: teaspoon

If you seldom serve soup but often make starters that require a knife and fork as below, it may be worth considering getting extra dessert knives and forks unless you don't mind washing up between courses. (If you have children, they are also invaluable for the years when they have grown out of baby cutlery but find full-size table knives and forks just a bit too big to cope with.)

Starter: dessert knife and dessert fork
Main course: table knife and table fork
Pudding: dessert spoon and dessert fork
Cheese: dessert knife
Coffee: teaspoon

Other cutlery

You might like to consider adding items such as a butter knife, a cheese knife, serving spoons and salad servers. Some couples would find steak knives very useful. Although they may be nice to have, fewer and fewer people go for fish knives and forks nowadays.

Miscellaneous tableware

This category covers any other decorative tableware, including napkins rings, salt and pepper mills, place card holders, candlesticks, wine coasters and tablemats. People love to buy silver so they are good items to include on your list.

Candlesticks/candles

The most traditional candlesticks are silver but candlesticks do come in the most enormous range of other materials including wood, pottery, glass and wrought iron. There are some beautiful crystal ones on the market and, again, some china companies do them to match their tableware.

If you prefer a more contemporary look to your table you could consider going for storm lanterns with thick cream candles or larger candles with several wicks, which look fantastic just sitting on a piece of glass or slate for example.

Napkin rings

To some people napkin rings are a total waste of time but to others they are completely essential. Silver napkin rings are the most traditional but there are literally hundreds of different styles on the market. Beaded napkin rings are widely available and very effective, but then so are napkins simply tied round with pretty ribbon. It is entirely a matter of personal choice what you decide to go for.

Place card holders

These are a fun addition to any table, and are the sort of present you might add to your list if you are keen on dinner-party entertaining. If that's not your style, cross it out now! They are small, usually silver plate, stands into which you put cards with your guests' names so everyone knows where they are sitting. Place name holders tend to come in sets of six in shapes such as apples or pheasants.

They are very useful if you are entertaining a group of people who may not have met one another before because it saves embarrassment if they can't remember each other's names!

Salt and pepper holders

The most practical choice is salt and pepper mills. The traditional (Capstan) shape comes in various materials from sterling silver to wood and acrylic.

Some people prefer to have a traditional salter with a spoon. These can usually be found in silver, glass or crystal. You could simply use a ramekin (custard cup) of salt with a very small spoon.

We tend to consider salt and pepper shakers to be rather old fashioned now and they are becoming harder and harder to find, though they are still part of some china ranges.

Tablemats

Traditional heat-resistant tablemats are often round or rectangular and come in every imaginable colour and design. Most ranges include place mats, coasters, serving mats and trays. You could choose completely plain mats for absolute safety, or perhaps plain with just a fine gold- or silver-coloured frame line. Or you might prefer those with pictures or patterns. It's very much a matter of personal taste.

Alternatives to the above are cotton or linen tablemats which come in various styles and colours. Cotton tablemats with matching or contrasting napkins are available in most stores, as are classic hemstitched linen tablemats, again with matching napkins.

Bear in mind that most place mats can easily be wiped clean, whereas if you go for linen or cotton, they have to be washed – and even then you may not be able to remove the red wine or blackcurrant jus!

Wine coasters

Silver wine coasters, which are sometimes known as wine slides, make a lovely wedding present. You can also buy beautiful glass or wooden coasters or other styles and designs.

A traditional wine coaster is about 13 cm (5 in) in diameter and is used as a stand for your wine bottle to avoid marking your table. It is worth having at least two so that you can have one at each end of your table or one for white wine and one for red.

Linen

The three types you will need to think about are table linen, bed linen and bathroom linen – towels to you and me!

Table linen
Nothing looks smarter than a dining table laid up with beautiful white linen. Although it is worth buying good quality, do be aware that in time it will stain, so you can't expect it to last forever. However, if you look after it, it should give you many years of service.

You might also like to ask for some bright and cheerful cloths for everyday use or for casual suppers.

Bed linen
Duvets and pillows
What quality of duvet and pillows to go for is a very personal decision. The main choices in natural fillings are duck feather and down, new white goose down, or new white Hungarian goose down. As you would expect, the quality of the filling is reflected in the price. New white Hungarian goose down is very popular because it is relatively lightweight and very warm. If you are prone to allergies you should definitely consider going for hollowfibre, which is a completely man-made filling.

The level of warmth that a duvet will give is measured by its 'tog' value. Most standard duvets are around 12 tog. One very popular option to have a 'combination' duvet. This is a pair of duvets, one 4.5 tog (for summer) and the other 9.5 tog (for autumn and spring). For winter they can be buttoned together to give a total tog value of 14.

If you are buying single duvets with children in mind it is not recommended to give them a higher tog value than 10.

Pillows come in all the same basic fillings as duvets and it is always worth having a couple of hollowfibre ones for your spare bed because it is amazing how many people have allergies to feathers.

Duvets and duvet covers come in superking, kingsize, double and single sizes. Pillows sizes are standard, square and bolster.

Duvet covers, sheets and pillowcases

Bed linen falls into three basic qualities: linen, cotton and polycotton.

Linen is fantastic but very expensive, with a double duvet cover costing well over £200. It also needs serious ironing. If you feel that linen is the only thing, why not consider having linen pillowcases and a cotton duvet cover and sheet?

Nowadays, 100 per cent cotton is the most popular choice for bed linen. It also needs to be ironed to look its best; the more patterned it is the easier it is to get away with putting it back on your bed unironed. But if you can't be bothered to iron at all, you could hide it under a throw or bedspread. There is a fantastic choice of 100 per cent cotton bed linen available from all kinds of sources. A lot of interior design companies have their own ranges, there are some very good specialist mail order companies, and all department stores also carry a good selection.

Polycotton is cheaper, doesn't need ironing unless you really want to, and can even be put back on a bed straight from the tumble dryer. Quality does vary considerably, and the really cheap options are a false economy.

A basic set of bed linen normally consists of a duvet cover, pillowcases (two per person) and a bottom sheet. Some people use a top sheet under the duvet on spare room beds so that when your guests leave you only have two sheets and some pillowcases to wash rather than having a cumbersome duvet cover to deal with.

Especially if you go for expensive bed linen that will last, choosing white or a plain, subtle colour is a good idea so it still looks stunning when you change your décor.

Bathroom linen

Good-quality towels are a real investment as they will last for many years. Most towels are made of either Egyptian or American cotton. American cotton tends to be slightly rougher than Egyptian cotton and it is a entirely a matter of personal choice which you prefer.

As far as choosing which colours to go for, it is probably wise to opt for classic tones such as white, cream, navy or bottle green, which will look fine in most bathrooms. When it comes

Choosing Your Wedding Presents ──────────

to deciding on quantities, go for as many as you feel you reasonably have room for.

Wrapping up in a great big bath sheet is wonderful when you have just stepped out of a hot bath. I like to give my visitors a bath sheet and a hand towel each plus a bath mat. I do, however, have the luxury of a tumble dryer, so washing and drying them isn't an issue. If you live in a small flat and washing bulky linen is difficult, most visitors who are staying for just one or two nights will cope perfectly well with a bath towel and a guest towel (a small hand towel) each.

> **Emma and Andrew**
> My client Emma was desperate to have turquoise towels to match the turquoise tiles in the bathroom of her rented flat. I put on my 'Mrs Interfering' hat and pointed out that she probably wouldn't live in the flat for very long and that she would be better to go for a more neutral colour that would look good in any bathroom. She agreed and was very glad she had because she and her husband came back from their honeymoon having decided to look for a property to buy.

Traditional/miscellaneous

Wedding guests love buying presents in this category. A lot of people think giving a single one-off wedding present is the ideal thing to do and the most traditional of all are items such as silver photo frames, crystal bowls and vases.

There are a lot of people whose opening words when telephoning to buy a wedding present are, 'I am not buying anything breakable or anything that is part of a set', immediately excluding a great chunk of the list! Bear in mind, though, that not everyone approves of wedding gift lists and those people are most likely to buy you things from this category.

These conflicting arguments mean you need quite a few items in this category on your list to give guests accessing the list plenty of choice of both larger and smaller items at a range of prices, and there's plenty of scope for that here. However, if you think a fair number of people will buy 'outside' the list, it may be best not to include too many of the obvious things.

Do think hard about your lifestyle and your longer-term plan before you complete this section of the list, though, and whether you need – or even like – some of these things. If you are never likely to go on a picnic, don't put a picnic hamper on your list, however much fun they look when you see them in the department store. It'll take up space and never go on an outing. If you're a backpacking and camping couple, large wheeled suitcases are not going to be on your most wanted list.

However, you might consider including smaller overnight or weekend luggage for the odd occasion when you stay overnight in a hotel – perhaps when invited to a friend's wedding!

> **Charlotte**
> There are some people who try to pass on their own unwanted presents, in which case you may be stuck with them until you are asked for something for the local charity tombola! One of my clients was given a silver bowl that she really didn't like but assumed was expensive as it was beautifully wrapped and in the carrier bag of a shop where she knew the guest shopped regularly. Charlotte decided to see if she could exchange the bowl for something she liked but was almost as embarrassed as the store manager, who had to explain that the bowl had been a free gift for spending over a certain amount of money with a cutlery company some years before!

Address book

If you are looking for an address book, why not consider going for a loose leaf one, i.e. one to which pages can be added or removed? People move house so much nowadays and it is great to be able to update your address book without it ever getting full. If you have friends who are constantly on the move, perhaps because they're in the armed forces, you can allocate them a page of their own and when it gets full just add another one.

Books
Many people choose to buy books such as dictionaries, atlases, cookery books and lifestyle/coffee table books. They are lovely things to have and particularly appeal to givers who would prefer not to buy china, glass or cutlery.

Luggage
When choosing luggage it is very important actually to see and lift the items in the shop and not to buy from a brochure. What looks like a nice lightweight suitcase in a picture can turn out to be a cumbersome piece of luggage that weighs a ton before you have even put a toothbrush in it.

When deciding which pieces of luggage to go for you will no doubt have your own thoughts. Some couples like one big suitcase that takes everything: others prefer a smaller suitcase plus a vanity case and a suit carrier. It is also worth considering adding a couple of weekend bags.

Nowadays most luggage ranges include pieces with wheels. If you have ever lugged a large case with no wheels off on holiday you will realise how invaluable this sort of suitcase has now become.

Photo frames

Photo frames are great wedding presents and are something that most people would consider giving. Don't put too many on your list because they are a classic example of a safe choice wedding present and you are quite likely to receive several from people who don't use your list.

I once had a client who had 11 guests that all thought, 'You can never go wrong with a nice silver photo frame'! In addition to their 11 she also received the four on her list – which, strangely enough, she decided to swap for something else.

Picnic hamper and rug

A traditional picnic hamper is a wicker chest with plates held in the lid by leather straps and glasses, food and drink held in the body of the hamper. This style of hamper is great if it's just going to live in the back of your car and not be carried any distance. However, if you are going off for a day in the country you are hardly going to want to lug such a cumbersome thing for miles. If you do decide to go for a traditional hamper, try to find one that has a handle at each end so that two people can carry it. In any event, it has to be a pretty big hamper to allow enough room for a decent picnic and most outings need a cool box as well, giving you more things to carry!

China plates will be much heavier and much less practical than melamine. They are also more difficult to pack up to take home when they are dirty – and more likely to break. Metal cutlery is also heavy, but you don't have to sink quite as low as plastic disposable knives, forks and spoons because melamine cutlery sets are a good compromise. You can also buy mugs and tumblers that are light and strong enough for picnicking but still attractive.

A popular alternative to a wicker hamper is an insulated back pack, sold either empty or with a variety of picnic items inside them – from salt and pepper shakers to acrylic wine glasses or tumblers. They are relatively light, easy to carry and keep your food and drink cool. A hugely practical recent option is an insulated pull-along hamper.

Strangely enough, quite a lot of people like to buy picnic rugs as wedding presents, especially if they buy 'outside' the list. In the unlikely event that you actually want one, the most practical option is to go for a waterproof-backed rug that folds up neatly with carrying handles.

Visitors' book

For some people a visitors' book is a complete waste of time but for others it becomes a lovely record of all the friends and family who have been to stay with you throughout your married life. Looking back through a visitors' book recalls memories of good times and can be just as evocative as flicking through a photograph album.

Most visitors' books are headed with Date, Name, Address and (sometimes) Comments at the top of each lined page.

Choosing Your Wedding Presents

Some people prefer not to have a comments column and others prefer to have a book with completely plain pages so that guests can write as little or as much as they like, or even draw the odd picture.

Toys and fun things

These presents obviously relate to your hobbies so you will be able to compile your own list fairly easily.

If you are an outdoor, walking, kayaking sort of couple you may decide you would like a complete set of Ordnance Survey maps, a pair of ultra-thin lightweight camping mattresses or a pair of silk sleeping bag liners. On the other hand, if you're more stay-at-home you could include 'toys' such as a Scalextric set or board games such as Monopoly or Trivial Pursuit.

You will probably find that these items are among the first things to be sold on your list as your guests will know that they will be well used throughout your married life.

General household

This includes items such as an electric drill, electric screwdriver, tool box, tools and a step ladder. Most people imagine that presents in this category are male orientated, but actually that's not necessarily the case. They are the sort of things that colleagues at work, who don't know the bride particularly well and aren't going to the wedding, may have a collection and buy.

Outdoor and garden

If you are lucky enough to have a garden, you may like to include either gardening equipment or perhaps some plants or garden furniture. This is another area where you can be imaginative, and give your guests plenty of choice.

Large items

Although there is nothing to stop you including sofas, beds and other large items of furniture on your wedding gift list, they tend not to be popular choices.

One idea is to ask for contributions or gift vouchers towards them. Some guests do not like the idea of this because they feel that if you do not get enough money to buy the item they have donated towards they then don't know what their money has been spent on. As a young person, given the choice of putting £40 towards a sofa for which the couple may not get the rest of the money anyway or buying them a nice vase or a stylish bread bin for the same amount, what would you do? At the other end of the scale, if you were spending £300 wouldn't you rather buy something that stands alone, like a lovely pair of silver candlesticks, than half a bed?

If your heart is set on listing such large items, bear in mind that you are quite likely to be given wedding present money and perhaps you could use this to make up any shortfall or simply to buy the item yourselves. It may well be that if you put any money you receive as wedding presents into a savings account

Choosing Your Wedding Presents

for a while, you will find that the shop in question has reduced the price of the sofa you want. It is definitely worth asking when compiling your list if any large item on it is likely to be in the sale at any time.

Difficult items

There are some items that you might as well expect to have to buy yourselves because they are notoriously difficult to get guests to choose. The first things that come to mind are mattress and pillow protectors – very unromantic! Also unpopular is anything of a similarly practical and essential, but boring, nature such as buckets and bowls, paint brushes and tea towels (dish cloths).

Perishable items are also not popular – wine, for example. As a guest once said to me, 'I'm not buying that. All that will happen is that they'll get drunk one night when they're having a party and the whole lot will just disappear without anyone appreciating what they are drinking.' If one of you really is a connoisseur of wine, it is worth considering having a separate wedding gift list with a firm of vintners.

The thought of asking your guests to make a donation to your favourite charity may be very appealing, but what most of your guests will want is to give *you* a present. If they want to give money to charity they will probably do it throughout the year anyway.

Chapter 8
Finalising Your Wedding Gift List

If you are dealing with a wedding list company, the final stage is to go through the list of 'promised' presents with them, confirming that you would like them to order everything on it, or making a few changes if you wish. This is called 'finalising'. Some couples feel that it is slightly unethical to swap or cancel presents and other couples have no qualms about it. There are some who are quite happy to be told the value of their wedding list and then effectively 'shop' from scratch. They may, for example, say that they wish to ensure they have all their main priority items and then see how much money is left for buying other presents. Then they can choose other presents to make up the value of their list irrespective of what their guests have actually chosen to give them.

In my opinion, I think it is courteous to consider your guests' feelings. If your grandma visits you every week and is likely to get real pleasure from seeing the vase she chose for you, it would be somewhat churlish to exchange it. On the other hand, imagine, you have been given a dozen whisky tumblers

Finalising Your Wedding Gift List

and a square spirit decanter by someone who didn't use your wedding gift list and you had exactly the same items on your list. When the guests who bought the tumblers and decanter through the list come to your house they will assume the crystal they see is the present they gave you and some people may not even comment on it. If they do say 'Is that the crystal we gave you?', crossing your fingers and saying yes is only a little white lie. Alternatively you could come clean and just say 'No, actually we were given that crystal by someone who didn't use our list so I hope you don't mind but we used the money from your present to make up our dinner service'.

Some guests wouldn't mind at all because they feel that the most important thing is that you get what you want. Others might strongly disapprove and be seriously put out that you decided not to accept the present they chose. How you deal with this is up to you, but in some cases being economical with the truth may be the best solution all round.

Obviously, the sooner you are able to finalise your list, the sooner your presents will be ready for delivery to you. Some couples like to finalise their wedding gift list before they go on their honeymoon: others prefer to do so after they get home and have had a chance to look at all the presents they received that were 'outside' their wedding gift list. This is the time when you have the opportunity to make up sets, cancel presents such as silver photo frames that have been duplicated by guests who haven't used your list, and also to buy any items you would like to purchase yourselves or using wedding present money.

Remember to ask the company that is administering your wedding gift list whether or not it gives a discount on any items you purchase yourselves.

Duplicates

If you do receive duplicate presents, you'll have to decide what you can and want to do about them. Most guests will be accommodating and be happy to give you the receipt so that you can exchange their gift for something else. You'll need to be tactful when you call them, but they are sure to want you to have something you will appreciate so are unlikely to be offended. If you really feel you cannot approach them, you may still be able to return the goods to a local store to exchange them if they will do so without a receipt. Failing that, you'll have to wait until you can give them to someone else, or stock-pile your second toaster for when the first one wears out!

Chapter 9

Delivery and Gift Wrapping

The way in which your presents are delivered will obviously depend on what sort of wedding gift list you decided to have. Indeed, the delivery options may well have been a factor way back when you were deciding how to administer your list in the first place.

Personal delivery

If your mother or another relative or friend is organising your list and the guests are buying the presents themselves, give some thought as to when you would like to receive them.

It is best to avoid having everyone arriving on the wedding day with armfuls of presents; your guests might expect you to open them on the spot and you just will not have the time. Ask them, instead, to deliver them before the wedding to your home or your parents' home, for example. Alternatively, invite them to visit you soon after the wedding to bring their gift.

Inevitably some guests will bring presents to the wedding, so give it a little advanced thought so you can forget about it on

Delivery and Gift Wrapping

the day. Delegate a couple of responsible people – perhaps ushers or bridesmaids – to take charge. Ask them to collect gifts from guests (this is often done at the end of the receiving line at the reception) and explain to them that you will open them after the wedding. Make sure there is somewhere secure to keep them during the reception, and that someone has taken responsibility for transporting and storing them safely until you can take delivery.

Whatever you do, don't think you'll remember who gave you what – even if you only leave it overnight once you have opened them. Your wedding day is far too exciting an event to allow your brain space for that kind of information!

Helen and Mike

Helen and Mike were staying the night at the hotel where they had had their wedding reception. They went to their room quite late and were delighted to find a complimentary bottle of ice cold champagne. Also there were all the presents guests who hadn't used their wedding gift list had brought to the reception.

'Hey,' said Helen, 'let's open the champagne and see what people have given us.' This was a big mistake. The next morning a somewhat bleary eyed Helen and Mike had to spend ages trying to rewrap their presents so that they could work out which paper and gift tag went with which present as neither of them could remember.

Delivery and Gift Wrapping

Using a store or wedding list company

If your list is with a store or you are working with a wedding list company, you have other options and it is generally better to have your presents delivered when you come back from your honeymoon. This gives you something to look forward to and also means that you are not going away leaving mountains of wedding presents still in their boxes lying around an empty house or flat. It is not unheard of for couples to come back from honeymoon to discover they have been burgled and everything is gone. Brand new wedding presents still in their original packaging are easily sold on.

Some companies, such as large department stores and smaller shops, may dispatch your wedding presents from stock as your list progresses, in which case you will be able to have them delivered at a suitable time and to a safe location. There may also be some items they have to order in specifically for you that won't be available until you return from your honeymoon. Keep in mind that most deliveries are likely to be attempted on Monday to Friday between 9 am and 5 pm when you may be out at work.

However, most specialist wedding gift list companies specifically order goods for brides once they have finalised their wedding gift list, which is after all your guests have made their choices and you have gone through the list and done any swapping around. This can mean that it takes longer for your presents to arrive but in the great scheme of things it is worth it.

Delivery and Gift Wrapping

Waiting a few extra weeks to get everything may mean you have a wider choice of presents in the first place and you have the opportunity to jiggle your list around a bit to avoid duplications.

There are companies who don't deliver anything until ten weeks after you have approved your list. At this point they deliver everything they have in stock but there may still be some presents to follow.

Some companies will order your china, glass, cutlery and other items with long lead times before your list is finalised but you may have to give them a credit card number and agree to pay for any items that are not sold through your list. If you are happy to do this it should certainly speed up delivery of your presents.

Make sure you know whether or not the shop or company running your list charges for delivery. Some wedding gift list services might charge as much as £4 to deliver the present.

Don't forget that, wherever you have your wedding gift list, you will also probably be able to go and collect your presents yourselves if that is more convenient.

Manufacturers' lead times

Most wedding gift list organisers will be able to give you manufacturers' lead times when you are compiling your wedding gift list. A lead time is the length of time between a company or shop placing an order and the goods being despatched by the manufacturer or supplier.

Delivery and Gift Wrapping

Remember, if you have been given lead times of eight to ten weeks for your dinner service to arrive, don't organise a party for the Saturday you get home from honeymoon or you could end up eating off paper plates!

There are a few reasons that can cause extensions to manufacturers' normal lead times and these are worth bearing in mind:

- Most factories have shut down/holiday periods at some time over the summer, Christmas and Easter, plus bank holidays.
- Certain items, such as covered vegetable dishes, may only be manufactured once a company has orders for a certain number. So you may get all your plates within the quoted lead time but have to wait longer for other pieces.

Household insurance

You will probably find that the value of your wedding presents is quite high and you should certainly check that your household contents insurance covers this increase in the value of your possessions. Be realistic about the amount of cover you have so that you are not under-insured should the worst happen.

A professional wedding gift list company should be able to give you a full retail value of your list.

Gift wrapping

People who give you their presents in person will obviously gift wrap them themselves, but most wedding list providers have a gift wrapping service that they will offer the buyer. The results are undeniably beautiful, but the service does come at a cost. The ultimate decision is, of course, the guest's and not yours but if you feel you don't want them to be tempted (or even pressurised) into this extra expense, you might feel able to express your preference on other grounds:

- You have chosen all the items on your wedding gift list yourself so do you really want your guests put to the additional expense of paying for wrapping paper that will be in the wastepaper basket within five minutes of your opening the gift?
- Most goods such as china, glass and canteens of cutlery come from the manufacturers in set quantities. For example, cutlery comes already neatly placed in its canteen. If enough individual guests buy place settings to make up a full canteen, why take it out for individual wrapping. It's possible for one place setting to go astray, but very unlikely that an entire canteen will be mislaid. The same is true of glasses: they frequently arrive from the manufacturers safely packed in boxes of six, but if three guests are each giving you a pair (which is how they are sold), why split the box and risk breakages?

Chapter 10

What to Do if Your Wedding is Cancelled

This will be a very short section as only a minute number of weddings are called off after the invitations have been sent out, so you are very unlikely to need this information. However, if your wedding is cancelled for any reason, all the presents you have received should be returned to the guests in question without delay. This will take time and energy, but it would be very unfair to keep the gifts under these circumstances.

You should return them by hand or by a secure route with a brief note of thanks and apology, and explain that the wedding has been called off. There is no need to give a reason unless you wish to.

If you are using a specialist wedding gift list company and have organised for your presents to be delivered after the wedding, you are likely to be expected to pay a fee to the company before they will refund the money to your guests. This may also be the case if a shop or company has already ordered in some of your presents.

What to Do if Your Wedding is Cancelled

Small individual shops or companies that have ordered goods specifically for you may also charge you a cancellation fee as they may well have to pay a restocking fee if they subsequently return the items to their supplier, and also to compensate them for the time they have wasted. Don't forget, they are in business and will not expect to pay for orders that have actually lost them money.

Chapter 11

With the Benefit of Hindsight

Hindsight is a very valuable thing and, if we had the chance, all of us would change some of the things we have done. Sometimes, however, we can benefit from other people's experiences. This chapter is based on interviews with four married couples talking about what they would do differently if they were getting married now. It may give you some ideas when you are thinking about what to include on your list.

Annie and Matthew

When Annie and Matthew got married eight years ago they didn't feel comfortable with the idea of having a wedding gift list. They felt it was rude and presumptuous and decided that they would be happy to accept anything their friends and family wanted to give them.

At the time of their wedding, they lived in a rented house and muddled through with an eclectic mixture of household items they had bought themselves or been given by other people.

They now own a house, have three children and still have the same mish-mash of household stuff plus more of the same that they received as wedding presents, some of which were: a large stainless steel tray and six martini glasses; a wooden tray with a breakfast set for two; an 18-piece everyday china set; two bath sheets and one hand towel in yellow; two bath sheets, two bath towels and two hand towels in bottle green; four bath towels and four hand towels in white; an 18-piece glasses set for red and white wine and champagne; a set of six red wine glasses; three square spirit decanters; two different sets of six whisky glasses; two different cut glass bowls; two silver photograph frames in completely different styles; lots of vases; a framed print (that wouldn't have been their own choice).

Individually, these could have been useful and thoughtful gifts, but collectively they added up to a lot of duplication and mismatches. What they would really like now is a decent set of china, a decent set of cutlery and a decent set of crystal!

'Our wedding presents were lovely but, though it sounds ungrateful to say it, they were fairly useless. We should definitely have put more thought into what to do about a wedding list. Even if we didn't put anything in with our invitations we should have compiled a list and given a copy to each of our mothers so that they could have guided those people who asked about presents in the right direction.

'As we have gone through our married life there have been so many necessary things – from large casseroles to pillows –

that we have had to go out and buy. Had we done some planning, we could have asked for them as presents. Having missed the opportunity to put a nice dinner service or a matching set of cutlery on a wedding list, we can't imagine when we are ever going to afford them. That is probably our biggest regret.'

Flora and James

Flora and James have now been married for ten years. They already had a house with most of the basics before their wedding.

They opted to have a wedding gift list with a department store and the bulk of it was made up of china, glass and cutlery. In addition they also had a few individual items like a deep-fat fryer, a visitors' book, and a round wooden cheese board with a glass dome that could also be used as a salad bowl. They put a note in with their invitations saying where their wedding gift list was held and sat back to see how things went.

Originally they put 12 place settings of everything on their list. When their list closed, none of their soup plates had been bought and they were still short of a few glasses. They were able to jiggle their presents around slightly so that they ended up with all the cutlery and 10 each of all their china and glass. In addition to this they were also given most of the individual items on their list.

They were slightly vague about who gave them what as far as their china, glass and cutlery was concerned but they knew exactly who have given them everything else on their list.

When asked if they are still happy with the presents they chose a decade ago they both said that there were two things they would have changed on the list. The first was their crystal, which they had chosen because it was the closest thing the department store in question stocked to what they had really wanted. The second was that they should never have bothered with a deep-fat fryer; it has been used twice in ten years!

Because of this, they said it would have been better if they had used an independent wedding list company so that they weren't restricted when it came to choosing their tableware to those manufacturers the store had access to. They also said that you should not list items – especially kitchen gadgets – that you are not sure you need.

Josie and Tom

Having only ever lived in fully furnished rental properties, Josie and Tom owned very little in the way of household belongings. When it came to the question of whether or not to have a wedding list they decided that they were leaving nothing to chance! They compiled a list, put the details in with their invitations and primed both sets of parents to steer anyone who thought they might do something a bit more individual straight back to the idea of buying from the list. Because they needed quite a lot of things they decided to go for one dinner service that would do for all occasions.

In retrospect they say there is very little they would change about their wedding gift list. They spent quite a lot of time compiling it and, three years on, can't think of anything they would change.

Hannah and Chris

This couple didn't need china, glass or cutlery but they desperately wanted a new sofa and chair. They decided to put these items on their list (held at a department store) along with some kitchenware, traditional presents and a small amount of linen.

They were given some, but not all, of the money they needed to buy the furniture so they decided to 'cash in' a few presents they felt they could buy themselves at a later date. They added the money to the present money they had been given and made up the small balance out of their own pockets.

Looking back, they are still happy with all the presents they received and say it was definitely the right decision to 'go the extra mile' themselves so that they got the sofa and chair. They knew their own priorities and decided to stick to them.

Chapter 12
Your Wedding Gift List

I have tried to include in this checklist all the items a couple might want to include on a wedding list so it can be used as a comprehensive starting point. Obviously everyone is different, so you'll need to go through it several times before you make it unique to you.

Start by deleting everything you are absolutely sure you don't need or want. If you are unsure, leave it there to start with and give it some more thought. Don't forget that you want to keep a good range of prices and types of gift on the list to give your guests plenty of choice. You should also include more gifts than you expect to receive – it's not very helpful if guests feel they don't have a choice if they don't look at the list until later.

It's also helpful to chat with other brides to see what decisions they made. They may be able to give you some useful tips.

Once you have narrowed it down to the items you would like to receive, start filling in the details of makes, colours and styles. Don't leave it to chance as even your closest friends can't read your mind and know instinctively what you want. Finally, work out your priorities so guests can be guided to what you would most like.

Your Wedding Gift List

Item	Quantity	Priority
Kitchenware		
Saucepans		
Double boiler		
Egg poacher		
Fish poacher		
Frying pan (skillet)		
Frying pan – large		
Milk pan		
Pressure cooker		
Saucepan – 16 cm (6½ in)		
Saucepan – 18 cm (7 in)		
Saucepan – 20 cm (8 in)		
Saucepan – 22 cm (8½ in)		
Sauté pan		
Steamer		
Stockpot		
Wok		
Casseroles (Dutch ovens) and oven-to-table ware		
Baking dish		
Casserole dish – 20 cm (8 in)		
Casserole dish – 24 cm (9½ in)		
Casserole dish – 28 cm (11 in)		
Flan dish		
Lasagne dish		
Ramekins (custard cups)		
Soufflé dish		

Your Wedding Gift List

Brand	Description

Your Wedding Gift List

Item	Quantity	Priority
Kitchen china		
Butter dish		
Cups and saucers		
Dessert/salad plates		
Dinner plates		
Egg cups		
Mugs		
Oatmeal bowls		
Pasta plates		
Serving dishes		
Side plates		
Soup plates		
Vegetable dishes		
Kitchen knives		
Carving fork		
Knife – 10 cm (4 in)		
Knife – 13 cm (5 in)		
Knife – 15 cm (6 in)		
Knife – 20 cm (8 in)		
Knife, bread		
Knife, carving		
Rack/block		
Sharpener/steel		

Your Wedding Gift List

Brand	Description

Your Wedding Gift List

Item	Quantity	Priority
Condiments		
Dressing jug/bottles		
Pepper mill/grinder		
Salt mill/grinder		
Baking equipment		
Cake tins (pans)		
Muffin pans		
Pie plates		
Roasting tin (pan)		
Yorkshire pudding tin (pan)		
Trays		
Other kitchen items		
Bread bin		
Bread board		
Cafetière		
Can opener		
Carving plate		
Cheese board and knife		
Chopping board		
Colander		
Cookery book		
Corkscrew		
Cream jug		
Dish drainer		

Your Wedding Gift List

Brand	Description

Your Wedding Gift List

Item	Quantity	Priority
Fondue set		
Garlic press		
Kitchen scales		
Kitchen scissors		
Ladle		
Measuring spoon		
Microwave cookware		
Milk jug		
Mixing bowls		
Pedal bin		
Potato peeler		
Rolling pin		
Salad bowl		
Salad servers		
Salad spinner		
Sieve (strainer)		
Spice rack		
Storage jars/tins		
Sugar bowl		
Teapot		
Tea strainer		
Timer		
Toast rack		
Trays		
Vacuum flask		
Vegetable rack		

Your Wedding Gift List

Brand	Description

Your Wedding Gift List

Item	Quantity	Priority
Washing up bowl		
Whisk		
Wooden spoons		
Electrical goods		
Alarm clock/radio		
Blender		
Bread maker		
Coffee grinder		
Coffee maker		
Deep-fat fryer		
Dust buster		
Electric blanket		
Electric carving knife		
Food mixer		
Food processor		
Hairdryer		
Ice cream maker		
Iron and ironing board		
Juicer		
Kettle		
Microwave		
Pressure cooker		
Radio		
Sandwich toaster		

Your Wedding Gift List

Brand	Description

Your Wedding Gift List

Item	Quantity	Priority
Sewing machine		
Slow cooker		
Standard lamp		
Stereo		
Table lamp		
Tea maker		
Telephone answering machine		
Television		
Toaster		
Video/DVD player		
Yoghurt maker		
White goods		
Cooker		
Dishwasher		
Freezer		
Fridge		
Spin dryer		
Tumble dryer		
Washing machine		
Vacuum cleaner		

Your Wedding Gift List

Brand	Description

Your Wedding Gift List

Item	Quantity	Priority
China		
Coffee cups and saucers		
Dinner plates		
Oatmeal bowls		
Salad/dessert plates		
Side plates		
Soup plates		
Teacups and saucers		
Serving pieces		
Butter dish		
Coffee pot		
Covered vegetable dish		
Cream jug		
Gravy boat and stand		
Meat plate		
Milk jug		
Open vegetable dish		
Oval platter		
Salt and pepper pots		
Sauce pot		
Soup tureen		
Sugar bowl		
Teapot		

Your Wedding Gift List

Brand	Description

Your Wedding Gift List

Item	Quantity	Priority
Glassware		
Beer glasses		
Brandy balloons		
Champagne flutes		
Highball glasses		
Goblets		
Port/liqueur glasses		
Red wine glasses		
Sherry glasses		
Tumblers		
Water glasses		
White wine glasses		
Port decanter		
Spirit decanter		
Wine decanter		
Water jug		
Cutlery		
Place settings		
Coffee spoons		
Dessert forks		
Dessert spoons		
Forks		
Knives		
Soup spoons		
Coffee spoons		

Your Wedding Gift List

Brand	Description

Your Wedding Gift List

Item	Quantity	Priority
Fish forks		
Fish knives		
Fruit knives		
Steak knives		
Teaspoons		
Other cutlery		
Butter knife		
Carving fork		
Carving knife		
Cheese knife		
Ladle		
Salad servers		
Serving spoons		
Miscellaneous tableware		
Candlesticks		
Coasters		
Mustard pot		
Napkin rings		
Pepper mill/shaker		
Place card holders		
Salt mill/shaker/trencher		
Serving mats		
Tablemats		
Wine coasters		

Your Wedding Gift List

Brand	Description

Your Wedding Gift List

Item	Quantity	Priority
Linen		
Table linen		
Tablecloth		
Napkins		
Bed linen		
Bedspread/throw		
Duvet		
Duvet cover		
Pillows		
Pillowcases		
Sheet		
Valance		
Bathroom linen		
Bath sheets		
Bath towels		
Face cloths		
Hand towels		
Bath mat		

Your Wedding Gift List

Brand	Description

Your Wedding Gift List

Item	Quantity	Priority
Traditional/miscellaneous		
Address book		
Ashtray		
Bathroom cabinet		
Bathroom scales		
Books		
Carpet sweeper		
Clock		
Clothes dryer		
Cocktail shaker		
Cushions		
Door mat		
House number/name plate		
House plants		
Fruit bowl		
Ice bucket		
Laundry basket		
Luggage		
Magazine rack		
Mirror		
Ornaments		
Photo album		
Photo frames		
Picnic hamper		
Picnic rug		
Picture/print		

Your Wedding Gift List

Brand	Description

Your Wedding Gift List

Item	Quantity	Priority
Rug		
Shower caddy		
Sofa throw		
Toilet roll holder		
Toothbrush holder		
Towel rail		
Umbrella stand		
Vase		
Visitors' book		
Wastepaper bin		
Wine cooler		
Wine rack		
Toys and fun things		
Board games		
Camcorder		
Camera		
Chess set		
Hobby equipment		
Sports equipment		

---- Your Wedding Gift List

Brand	Description

Your Wedding Gift List

Item	Quantity	Priority
General household		
Burglar alarm		
Door chains		
Door locks		
Electric drill		
Electric screwdriver		
Smoke detectors		
Step ladder		
Tool box		
Tools		
Window catches and locks		
Outdoor and garden		
Barbecue		
Barbecue accessories		
Garden furniture		
Garden lighting		
Gardening tools		
Hedge trimmer		
Hose reel		
Lawn mower		
Plants/shrubs/trees		
Strimmer		
Washing line		
Wheelbarrow		

Your Wedding Gift List

	Brand	Description

Your Wedding Gift List

Item	Quantity	Priority
Large items		
Bed		
Bedside table		
Bookcase		
Chairs		
Dining chairs		
Dining table		
Sofa		
Wardrobe		
Difficult items		
Buckets and bowls		
Charitable donations		
Decorating equipment		
Dustpan and brush		
Floor mop and broom		
Mattress protector		
Pillow protectors		
Tea towels (dish cloths)		
Wine		

Your Wedding Gift List

Brand	Description

Wedding Gift List Companies

Specialist wedding list companies

Onslow & Ridley
John Player Building, Stirling, FK7 7RP
Offices: Edinburgh and Cromlix, Perthshire
Telephone: 08717 344041
E-mail: weddinglists@onslowandridley.co.uk
Website: www.onslowandridley.co.uk

Wedding List Direct
47 Heythorp Road, Southfields, London, SW18 5BS
Telephone: 020 8874 7908
E-mail: lesley@weddinglistdirect.co.uk
Website: www.weddinglistdirect.co.uk

Wedding List Services
127 Queenstown Road, London, SW8 3RH
Telephone: 020 7384 8484
Website: www.wedding.co.uk

Wedding Presents Direct
Unit 2, Standen Manor Farm, Hungerford, Berkshire, RG17 0RB
Telephone: 01488 662100
E-mail: office@weddingpresentsdirect.co.uk
Website: www.weddingpresentsdirect.co.uk

Wedding Gift List Companies

The Wedding Shop
171 Fulham Road, London, SW3 6JW
Telephone: 020 7384 8400
Website: www.theweddingshoponline.co.uk

Department stores offering wedding list services

National stores

Argos
Argos Direct, Acton Gate, Stafford, ST18 9AR
Telephone: 08706 003030
E-mail: info@argos.co.uk
Website: www.argos.co.uk

Debenhams
Customer Relations, Debenhams Retail plc, 1 Welbeck Street, London, W1G 0AA
Telephone: 020 7408 4444 (head office);
08702 424555 (wedding stationery)
Website: www.debenhams.com

House of Fraser
Website: www.houseoffraser.co.uk

John Lewis
Website: www.johnlewis.com

Marks & Spencer
Website: www.marksandspencer.com

Wedding Gift List Companies

Independent stores

GTC (London)
2 Symons Street, Sloane Square, London, SW3 2TJ
Telephone: 020 7730 0411
Website: www.general-trading.co.uk

Harrods (London)
87–135 Brompton Road, Knightsbridge, London, SW1X 7XL
Telephone: 020 7730 1234
Website: www.harrods.com

Jenners (Edinburgh)
48 Princes Street, Edinburgh, EH2 2YJ
Telephone: 01312 25 2442
Website: www.jenners.com

Liberty (London)
32 Kingly Street, London, W1R 5LZ
Telephone: 020 7573 9652
Website: www.liberty.co.uk

Selfridges (London)
Telephone: 08708 377377
Website: www.selfridges.co.uk

Index

address books 72–3

baking equipment 50–1
bathroom linen 69–70
bed linen 67–9
books 73
  address books 72–3
  visitors' books 75–6
bread bins 51
bride's mother 6, 8, 11–13, 27

cancellation of wedding 88–9
candlesticks 64
casserole dishes 44–6
cast iron
  oven-to-table ware 44–5
  saucepans 44
chief bridesmaid 11–13
china 54–60
  kitchen china 46–8
  pattern 55–6
  place settings 58–9
  price 55
  quantities 57
  serving pieces 59–60
coasters 66
company gift lists 15–17, 21–2
  delivery 84–6
  finalising 79–81
  updating 27
condiments 50, 65
cups 47, 59
cutlery 62–3

delivery of gifts 14, 15, 17, 18, 82–7
departmental store lists 13–14, 21–2, 27
dinner services *see* china
duplicated gifts 79–81
duvets 67–8

e-mail 30
electrical goods 51–4

food processors 52

garden gifts 77
gift lists
  company services 15–17, 21–2
  deciding on type 20–2
  departmental store 13–14, 21–2
  finalising 79–81
  individual shops 17–18, 21–2
  informing guests about 23–5
  internet services 18–19, 21–2, 27
  length of 36–7
  and mother of bride 11–13, 27
  need for 5–6, 7–10
personal 11–13, 27
planning 33–40
price range 9–10, 37–8
prioritising 38, 39
updating 26–8
gifts
  delay in receiving 15, 17, 18,
  delivery 14, 15, 17, 19, 82–7
  difficult items 78
  large items 77–8
  received at the wedding 82–3
  researching 41–2
  returning 88–9
  wrapping 87
glassware 60–1
guests
  considering needs of 20, 71
  expenditure on gifts 8, 9–10, 37–8
  influencing choices 26
  informing about list 23–5
  see also thank-you letters

127

Index

hobbies 76
household items 76

insurance 86
internet
  company services 15–17
  departmental stores 13–14
  online lists 18–19, 21–2, 27
invitations
  including details of gift list 23–5

kettles 52–3
kitchen china 46–8
kitchenware 42–51
knives 48–50, 63

lead times 15, 17, 85–6
linen 67–70
luggage 73

master list 11–13
microwave ovens 53
money 77–8
mugs 47

napkin rings 64

outdoor gifts 77
oven-to-table ware 44–6

pasta plates 47
personal lists 11–13
  updating 27
photo frames 74
picnic hampers 74–5
pillows 67–8
place card holders 65

place settings
  china 58–9
  cutlery 63
planning 33–40
presents *see* gifts
price range 9–10, 37–8
prioritising 38, 39

ramekins 45–6
researching gifts 41–2, 54

salt and pepper 50, 65
saucepans 42–4
shops
departmental store lists 13–14, 21–2, 27
individual store lists 17–18, 21–2, 27
steamers 44

table linen 67
tablemats 66
tableware 64–6
  see also china; cutlery
thank-you letters 29–32
toasters 53
towels 40, 69–70
toys 76
traditional presents 71–6

updating lists 26–8

visitors' books 75–6

washing machines 54
wedding cancellations 88–9
Which? Online 41
white goods 54
wine coasters 66